Improving Sex in Marriage

By Gary Hall

Part One - Getting to Know Each Other Intimately
Introduction

There are great reasons why spouses need to talk to each other about sex, and how to make it better in their marriage. Hot, amazing, satisfying sexual relations makes better almost every aspect of daily life. Sex acts as a natural mood enhancer. Performance improves at work, and energy levels rise when a marriage has a thriving sexual component to it.

Blood pressure maintains normal limits. For someone who has high blood pressure, the antidote may be a regular dose of deep and satisfying lovemaking. Blood glucose levels are also positively affected, and mineral levels in the bloodstream stabilize.

A regular dose of sexual intimacy brings harmony to a marriage. Stressful issues, money, paying bills, rent and mortgage all sap the strength out of an otherwise loving relationship. Bickering and fighting over money leads to finger pointing, arguments and resentment.

A marriage with a thriving sexual component softens the stress associated with daily life. Daunting financial issues can be solved with teamwork and mutual understanding, and the togetherness couples feel when they relieve stress with bedroom intimacy.

Driving in heavy traffic is frustrating. Everyone has had incidents of road rage. Repressing anger is unhealthy for the body but is diffused during a passionate session of sex, when both partners can release all the tension that built up during the day.

Psychological issues like depression and anxiety become less chronic, and depressed mental states occur with less frequency when married partners are sexually active. Affection, cuddling, kissing the body often provides an antidote for a partner feeling down or anxious.

Stripping naked and taking a bath together soothes the muscles and also stimulates sex drive. Couples sitting a hot tub can relax together naked, letting the jets pulsate against tired muscles. A man lifts up his wife on top of him, her body light in the water, and have stimulating underwater sex.

The human body was built for sex. Many species in the animal kingdom mate only during certain periods of the year, but humans engage in sex year-round. Sex is the antidote in marriage for most common problems that arise, and it can be performed as often as necessary.

The European view of sexuality is considered more "mature," and "grown up," in comparison to America. But every man and woman both in Europe or America, and the rest of the world for that matter, have the same urges and desires to have pleasurable and satisfying sex.

Married couples have the safest way to engage in sex. It's also the most economical, although going out to a restaurant or buying gifts to your lover works wonderfully to communicate a partner's interest in intimacy that night. The main reasons why sex in a marriage is usually the best sex one can have is:

- You and your partner know each other and have shared intimate secrets
- Exploring sexuality by experimenting can be done safely
- Sex without love or affection usually ends up with feelings of regret or dissatisfaction

Chapter 1
Finding Love

Sex without love is as hollow and ridiculous as love without sex."
— *Hunter S. Thompson*

Anyone who is observant, who discovers the person they have always dreamed of, knows that sexual energy comes into play before sex even takes place. The greatest pleasure isn't sex, but the passion with which it is practiced...
— *Paulo Coelho*

Have you ever had a sexual fantasy where you meet a lover in a secret place in the dark of night? Once alone and safe from prying eyes, you enjoy a night of hot and passionate sex, and your lover's skill releases your carnal lust and satisfies your deepest sexual desires. You will remember that night forever.

The hottest selling books throughout the history of book publishing are romance novels, and its subcategory, erotica. Typically, these stories involve a female who catches the eye of a gorgeous, virile man. He may be a billionaire, and he may be impetuous. They meet, but a conflict arises that threatens their blossoming relationship. The conflict is resolved, usually with lots of drama. They reunite at the end and have a deep and intensely satisfying sexual relationship and live happily ever after.

Romance novels are a wonderful escape and fit perfectly within a marriage. They serve an important role of stimulating the imagination. The fantasy world in these books, erotic and lustful, are seeds that can grow and help take sexual relations to the next level.

The partner you married is the person you fell in love with. Over the years, marriage becomes comfortable and predictable. Often the initial spark dies out at the same time each partner makes significant progress in their careers. Partners draw the conclusion that the romantic spark must be sacrificed in order to be successful. Friends and acquaintances have the same experience, confessing their love lives at home are not as thrilling as they once were. The greater the success, the more the sex life in marriage suffers.

Bars and nightclubs provide places a disaffected marriage partner often goes in the hope of meeting someone who will reignite that spark. These places provide an atmosphere which promotes encounters with strangers, and profit from providing a place for these encounters.

The truth is that sometimes, a marriage partner will have success meeting someone who can understand them, relate to them, and make them feel loved. In reality, however, a positive and life changing encounter after meeting someone in a club is extremely rare.

Speed dating works on first impressions. People only have a few minutes to "make a connection." Common sense tells us it is next to impossible to know someone enough in a few minutes to make an informed decision.

Some dating apps boast of their ability to match you with someone with whom you belong based on key personality profile indicators. In truth, research shows that only a very low percentage of partners have a long and fruitful relationship based on their profiles.

Despite the rise of social media, dating sites and texting, people are in fact more socially isolated than ever before, spending lonely nights at home alone in front of the computer, talking with "friends" they've never met nor will meet any time in the future.

Despite the revolution in communication, you have a better chance of meeting a person who can understand and satisfy you emotionally and physically, through a chance, in person encounter. Or a blind date, or someone you met and fell in love with in high school or college. Or bumping into them in the library, the supermarket, the laundromat, or someone you meet at work. It has been this way for tens of thousands of years (even before the idea of laundromats ever existed). When it comes to love, compatibility and sex, is there nothing new under the sun?

In the final analysis, it is always wisest to try to keep a marriage strong and make it last a lifetime. Exploring unknown heights and depths of sexuality between married partners, trying new sex positions, role playing, foreplay, teasing and giving to each other what they ask for in sex, will raise the bar and bring about the best sex couples can have. With openness, sex between married partners can compete successfully with the sexual fantasies described in the wildest romance novels.

Sex in Marriage

Sexual thoughts and carnal desires start in the brain's limbic system, the oldest and least understood part of the brain. The rules of attraction can't be quantified or be understood by an algorithm no matter what you're told. It is best to think of sex as one of the healthiest experiences a human can participate in. Sexual feelings and the desire for intimacy are the most natural thoughts humans can have.

Have you ever seen a married couple in public who seem happy and are playful with each other? They enjoy each other's company and seem carefree and easygoing. They genuinely seem to like each other. People smile knowingly at such people, imagining they have a fulfilling sex life together, and will spend years happy in the company of each other.

There's no reason why sex in marriage needs to be dull. Sex can and should be dynamic, exciting and gratifying. Just because your partner's body has become familiar does not mean that sex has to be predictable and unimaginative. Realistically speaking, partners in a 15-year marriage may actually know only 10% of each other's body. Get to know your partner's body and make new discoveries about each other. Tap into their libido and their lustful thoughts.

Do you know all your partner's erogenous zones? Have you tried every sexual position there is? Was there a time once, in bed, where you tried role playing, one partner taking the dominant role and the other submissive, who must obey every word his or her Master dictates? This is an example of role playing.

Have you ever teased your partner into an explosive orgasms, without penetration? Your partner's body is an undiscovered country. Partners should be explorers, discovering along the way that *every inch* of your lover's body is an erogenous zone. Husbands and wives can learn how to entice, titillate and arouse all areas of their bodies.

Great sex is one of the best ways to stay fulfilled in marriage. Talking to each other about it is critical to a sexually satisfying relationship. Communication is key between long term partners. Spouses should be able to talk openly about their sexual feelings, and also about what they feel is missing. There are ways to communicate these concerns without hurting feelings or making your loved one feel inadequate in some way.

When you talk things out, and are able to share the most private and secret sexual yearnings, you pave the way to better and more satisfying sex

Most relationships began because two people were attracted to each other. Sexual thoughts and desire for the each other started immediately. Over time, the affection you had for your partner and your desire to be intimate grew more intense. In marriage you were able to release all the desire that had been building up.

When you're in love, love and sex are one and the same. In a clandestine affair, there is often sex and no love. The sexual experience is completely different. Lustful feelings of the body and mind are satisfied, but the sense of completeness – sex and love combined – is missing.

Improving sexual relations in a marriage last through the life of the marriage. It is the glue which keeps the marriage relationship strong and healthy. Caring for each other and helping each other are one and the same as sharing your body with your loved one intimately.

Chapter 2
Knowing your Partner Intimately

Sex is always about emotions. Good sex is about free emotions; bad sex is about blocked emotions.
-Deepak Chopra
"Many lovers are 'off to the races:' hurtling towards orgasm, they miss the excitement of sensual meanderings along the way."
— Alexandra Katehakis

What, in your view, is the best part of sex? Men, is it when you are penetrating your partner, listening to her moan with pleasure as she moves closer and closer to orgasm with each thrust of your penis? She's having what seems like an out of body experience, soft moans turn to yelling so loud you cover her mouth so the neighbors won't hear?

Or maybe that first sight of her when she sits down next to you, wearing a tight shirt as her breasts bounce a little and she knows you're checking her out and her smile says, "Let's go to the bedroom and get it on?"

Women love knowing their partner admires them for their mind and for their body. A woman's power comes from her ability to entice and seduce her man. Aphrodite was the goddess of love, beauty and sexual passion in Greek mythology. Every woman can harness the seductive, sexual power talked about in mythology.

The Physiology of Orgasm

Men achieve orgasm usually through sexual intercourse. Research in human sexuality theorizes that men orgasm through intercourse in order to achieve reproductive success. Men are under "selective pressure" to ejaculate so they can propagate the species.

Simply put, men are hardwired to mate and impregnate females. While this sounds like a cold, antiseptic explanation, it helps to understand how men are sexually satisfied. But the sexual role of men in marriage is much more complex than simply taking his wife, delivering his seed and then going to sleep.

A woman's orgasm is less understood, and later there will be a detailed discussion of the subject. In general, most women can achieve orgasm through clitoral stimulation. Other women can orgasm through vaginal sex, and even others through both clitoral stimulation and vaginal sex. Some sex positions satisfy a woman more than others, because these positions involve vaginal and clitoral stimulation simultaneously.

Women traditionally seek a mate to bear children and to provide in one way or the other to help build shelter in which to raise children. Women have also been chastised for talking openly about their sexuality.

Marriage Vows and What they mean in Terms of Marital Sex
Marriage is a contact, an agreement. Recall your marriage vows. Vows have historically been adapted from the Bible, but in recent years they have changed. Some couples recite secular vows. Perhaps the best marriage vows come from the Old Testament:

Ephesians 5:25: "For husbands, this means love your wives, just as Christ loved the church. He gave up his life for her."

Genesis 2:24: "Therefore a man shall leave his father and his mother and hold fast to his wife, and they shall become one flesh."

Biblical marriage vows refer both to loving and supporting one another and also male and female sexuality. A man must love his wife and also satisfy her. Women achieve sexual satisfaction much differently than men. The primary area of sexual stimulation is not the vagina. It is the clitoris. There is distance between a woman's clitoris and her vaginal opening. In order for most women to achieve orgasm during sex, her clitoris must be stimulated.

We will discuss later the best sexual positions couples can do to stimulate the clitoris while at the same time stimulating the male partner during intercourse. There are other positions that clearly satisfy women more than men, and vice versa.

What does satisfying a women have to do with marriage vows? The answer is found in the phrase *Love your wives.* A man in marriage should help provide for the household, provide protection for his family. But he must also "love his wife." For our purposes, we will modify it to *Make love and satisfy your wives.*

While a man in marriage has the responsibility to satisfy his wife, women are also responsible to please and satisfy their husbands. The best sex is when both partners are satisfied, and this can be achieved through openness and by knowing what stimulates and excites your partner.

Female Sexuality

One scientific study remarked that it is rare for females of any species to achieve orgasm solely through sexual intercourse. This is due to the location of the clitoris and its distance from the vaginal opening. However, some women have reported achieving orgasm through sexual intercourse without clitoral stimulation.

Women, then, must first learn how to orgasm. They can do this on their own. Masturbating is a great way to discover what it takes to achieve a deep and satisfying orgasm. Then, when a woman has sex with her husband, they perform sexual positions that stimulate the same way it felt when masturbating.

When it comes to sex, for some women it is not always about achieving orgasm. When a woman feels loved and protected, she experiences well-being. Well-being is an arousal state, which will blossom into sexual arousal through her love of the man who loves her back. Switching from well-being arousal to sexual arousal occurs in a fraction of a second.

Sexual arousal in a woman may begin before foreplay and sex. A woman who is in love with her husband can watch him performing any kind of task, from talking on the phone to replacing a light bulb to washing the car. She watches him and thinks about the last time she and her husband were intimate together. She can turn on when she fantasizes about the physical sensations she felt, the feeling of his lips pressed against hers, the scent of his body, the sweat of his body on her when he was on top and sharing his satisfaction when he orgasmed.

Male cleanliness is important to many married women. Perspiring all day, with or without physical labor, women appreciate a man who bathes before sexual intercourse, preferring the fresh, clean smell of soap instead of dank sweat.

Male Sexuality

Men think about sex much differently than women. A man may be dormant one moment, hand the next switch to arousal when he's either visually stimulated or through touch. Women can maintain an arousal state for hours without the arousal being specifically sexual in nature. Because of the strong visual component of male arousal, there are many forces in society, especially the media which will grab the attention of males, usually to sell them some product.

The visual aspect of males may have an evolutionary basis, going back to pre-civilization when primates and early humans lived in hunter-gatherer societies. Men who hunted needed to spot and capture their prey.

It is of no surprise that all kinds of media have exploited the visual basis of men's sexuality. Pornography is immensely popular, and most viewers of porn are men, although there is a rise in the number of women who watch adult films. The visual aspect of pornographic videos focuses men on sex.

Advertisements for beer, marketed almost exclusively to men, usually feature a young, attractive, well-developed female holding a beer bottle or standing next to a six pack. It is not unusual to see pictorial advertisements for upcoming car races in America of a woman dressed in revealing cutoff jeans and a tight half top leaning over a racing car suggestively. But the woman and the car races have nothing at all in common.

There are other ads targeted at men that have nothing at all to do with women, yet a picture of a scantily clad woman accompanies the product or service advertised. Gambling ads often feature women whose expressions suggest she is sexually available to the man who will risk his money in the gambling casino.

These distractions can do one of two things for a marriage: the husband can be drawn into the illusion that there is something better than what his wife offers him at home, disrupting his marriage. Or it can fuel the married couple's sexual life and make it more satisfying by introducing fantasy into the marriage through role playing and experimentation.

Married men admire women who take care of themselves, and who can stimulate both mentally and visually. We'll discuss further what each partner can do to have a deeply satisfying sexual relationship.

CHAPTER 3
Girl Talk

First and foremost, because of the powerful role women play in intimacy and in a marriage, *never use sex as a weapon.* When a man is denied even one time, he remembers it, and the seeds of resentment are sowed and can last for weeks, months or even years. Instead of denying sex, the best way to avoid this situation is by removing oneself from the argument or disagreement, *before* a denial occurs.

Walk away and gather yourself. Take a deep breath and try to put what is happening in perspective. Ask if the disagreement really matters in the big picture. Even better, try to understand why your husband feels the way he does. Reminding oneself of her love for her husband and the disagreement, may turn out to be a misunderstanding. Return to the scene of the argument and talk it out. Try and make a compromise.

There is an old Hebrew saying that married couples should never go to bed angry, and there is a great deal of truth in that. For both partners, it is important to learn to forgive. If a woman has the capacity to forgive small and insignificant things, the sexual milieu at home will grow stronger. Instead of a house of disagreements and bickering, it should be the place where affection and healthy sexual desire can manifest.

Husbands and "The Male Gaze"

Men are visual creatures and respond to attractive women. A wife doesn't need to dress up like a supermodel every minute of the day, nor does she need to wear a dress when cleaning dishes in the kitchen or vacuuming the living room.

Women should know what their husbands find most attractive in them. If his first complement on your body before marriage was your shapely, pretty legs, it's great to show them off whenever you can. When a wife advertises her assets, she sends a silent but powerful communication to her husband. Feminine beauty and sexual appeal transmits the dual message of power and availability. You have the gaze of your husband which is a controlling force, and you also convey that you are there for him to take.

So much of sex is playing. A light attitude is always conducive to intimacy. If a woman's husband has complemented her breasts, she can wear a top that shows off her cleavage. When she bends down to speak or ask a question, she can see her partner's eyes drift down from her face to her physical assets. Teasing and playing can be fun, while it transmits a woman's sexual power over her husband. Spouses know they are in their husband's gaze. To set a mood, wear sexy underwear, a little perfume, and a cute outfit which displays her best assets. You can use speak in a silent language, conveying your desire.

Building Sexual Tension. First Scenario

Women are at the controls when it comes to sexual encounters in marriage, whether they know it or not. A women has the ability to have sex cool, lukewarm, or steamy and hot. Here is a short story which demonstrates her ability to turn up the heat.

It's Saturday morning. You both have the day off. You wake up to find your husband is up and out of bed already. You feel disappointment, because when you woke you thought about what happened last night, when your husband and you engaged in spontaneous, passionate sex that came as a complete surprise. You did it just before going to sleep, and you remember how good it felt, how he held you tightly to him and penetrated you, thrusting harder and harder until finally, he exploded with a powerful orgasm. He patiently waited for you after and tried helping you finish. You mounted him but for some reason, you got close, but couldn't go all the way. You slept well, but there was something missing.

You're alone in bed and you wanted him this morning. He's out of bed and you don't know what he's up to. You gently stroke your clitoris and feel jolts of pleasure run through your body. Your desire is building now. You get up and walk to the closet to get your robe. But an idea comes to you and you take off what you're wearing and wrap the robe around your naked body.

You walk out of the bedroom and don't see your husband, but you hear a noise coming from outside. You realize he is in the garage, so you walk through the kitchen and don't see any empty coffee cups, or anything that he been prepared to eat.

You know he likes coffee in the morning, so you prepare it in the coffeemaker. He likes toast, so you put two slices in the toaster. You take out the spread he likes. But the last thing you want is for him to take a sip of the coffee or a bite of the toast. You're setting a trap. The kitchen is nice and warm and you feel good in your nakedness under the robe. You touch your breast gently and run your finger over a nipple, sending a gentle jolt of pleasure down your body to your genitals. The aroma of brewed coffee wafts through the air. You walk to the garage door and open it, and your husband is there working. You leave the door open a little and walk away to see if he picks up the smell.

You are pleased with the trap you've set. In the meantime, the toast pops up in the toaster and you take it out and apply the spread with a butter knife and set it on a plate on the counter. Now the coffee has brewed. Whether he responds to the coffee smell or not, it's time that he joins you in the kitchen.

You wait half a minute. He's still out there, so you walk over to the door. Before you call to him you loosen a couple of buttons on the robe, revealing only a little of your round cleavage.

"Good morning. Coffee's ready in the kitchen."

He looks up and sees you and his gaze stays on you an extra few seconds. You watch as his eyes scan your robe and focuses on the open area you unbutton and exposed.

"I made you some toast too."

"Oh, great. I'll be right in."

You decide to stand by the kitchen sink, busying yourself with anything you can get your hands on. He comes in the door and walks up to you from behind, rests his hands on your shoulders, bends down and kisses your cheek. You respond and press your cheek against his hand, keeping it there for a few moments.

He takes a step to the coffeemaker and begins pouring himself a cup. Now you turn to face him, letting some more of your robe separate itself.

"How'd you sleep last night?" You ask softly, in a quiet voice tinged with just a sprinkle of sexuality. As you face him, he sees your robe is open a few more inches. It's now clear to him you have nothing on underneath.

His eyes move up and down your body and you see it finally registers. He glances at your face and sees you smiling at him. You don't need to say a word, because you already sent a silent message that tells him what you want.

You don't want to take off your robe, you want your lover to do that. But you help out by parting it a little more as you take a step towards him. His eyes widen as he scans your body, your soft skin, your feminine essence. You take a quick look down at his crotch and see a little lump that tells you that it's begun.

You go near him and press your body to his, and you hand reaches down to take hold of his dick. You squeeze it and let your fingers linger on it, enough to let him know you want him right now. You look up and you embrace.

His soft lips on your lips with its one million nerve endings, arouses you more. Wetness courses down between your legs. You want to rip off his clothes and have him fuck you like mad, but you restrain your lust. In order for this to work you need to go slowly. You have him, and his penis is getting bigger. He presses into you now, and your body warms from the feel of his chest against yours.

You need to decide, do you want to unzip his pants, bend down and suck his cock? Is he completely hard now? Or do you want to be romantic, look at him and help him take off his clothes, then embrace more? Where do you want to do it, right here in the kitchen or in the bedroom? Both?

You decide you want it right here and now. There's unfinished business from last night, and the urge to explode is already building inside you. You want it right here. You won't suck him, because he's already hard. In fact, he's pressing it into you.

The first thing to do is release the pressure in his pants. You smile at him and silently communicate that you will do the work, but he'll owe you for it. Now you unbuckle his belt and unzip him, pull down his pants below his knees, followed by his boxer shorts.

Out pops his magnificent dick, magnificent not because it looks nice, but because of the pleasure it always provide to you. You take it in your hand, lift it a little and stroke it. Your lover's breathing harder, feeling pleasure from the feel of your hand on him and how you stroke it over his sensitive part just below the tip.

You feel its warmth in your hand. The thickness. He reaches into your robe to feel your nakedness, wraps his arms around your waist and hips and gently pulls you closer to him. You stop stroking but keep your grip as his hands slide around your back, moves down and takes hold your buttocks. He begins breathing harder as his hands move faster over your skin. You are now in Act Two, working up to the final act.

His hands move up your back and around the front as his fingers brush over your nipples. A hand remains on your breast and he squeezes it, sending a jolt of pleasure down between your legs. You've stopped stroking him again, but you've gripped it tighter, and feel the blood pulsing through his stiff, hard cock.

Act Three is about to begin and the only question remaining is, where will we do it? But you can't wait to answer, because you are caught up in the intense pleasure of his lips on your tit, gently biting your nipples, your neck, his hands squeezing your buttocks. You could stay like this forever, except for releasing that pressure you've had in you since last night.

You decide it's time. He kisses your ear and you feel his hot breath blowing in it, and you get goose bumps. At any other time, his breath in your ear would make you ticklish, but right now it's sending waves of desire all through your tingling, waiting body.

Your lips are at his ear. "Fuck me," you breathe into it. "Fuck me." You make the first move. You turn towards the sink; no longer aware your robe is pulled apart but still on you. He stands behind you now, takes your robe in his hands and pulls it off you quickly. You spread out your arms to assist.

He presses his hard dick into your naked back and grinds it, and your hips start moving on their own. You have him doing now what you always wanted him to do, taking control. He runs his hands between your legs, his fingers rub your clitoris, stroking it between your legs, running his fingers over the labia of your vagina. He's checking to see if you're ready to take him inside you.

He presses your back forward and down and spreads your legs a little. Your clit presses against a kitchen towel, a fortunate coincidence. He's moving his hands quickly, through your legs, over your buttocks, around the front and squeezing your breasts. You're getting wetter and wetter, feeling it gushing out between your legs.

He has you bent over and you know him and you know how excited he is. You've done this innumerable times before, but never this way. Never in the kitchen. And you love how aggressive he is with you. You're breathing hard and losing patience. You already told him to fuck you, didn't you? What's he waiting for? Finally, he's spreading your legs and has gripped his cock. Moving it up and down your drenched pussy. He's searching and has found it as you feel his tip at your opening. His hands grip your hips, and then...

There is nothing in the world like the feeling when he first penetrates you. It always feel new and surprising the first time he pushes in. His member stretches out your vaginal walls, and the feeling is impossible to put into words. It goes into that deep spot inside you. It's started.

He thrusts into you, moving you back and forth, squeezing your hips as if you were a rag doll. He thrusts harder than you've felt in a long time, and you hear him grunt softly behind you. Your clit rubs against the towel with each thrust, taking you higher and higher. Your eyes are closed and all that exists is the intense sensation that starts between your legs and moves up through your body. You're not aware that you're moaning louder and louder with each thrust. Then there's a surprise. He reaches one hand around you and in front. He pulls you away from the sink a little so he can rub your clit with his finger as he's fucking you.

His finger rubbing was what was needed to take you over the edge, and to finally reach for release. You are nothing, no arms, hands, breasts, legs. You are only the sensation. It starts deep inside you, somewhere just below your navel. It grows and grows, getting bigger and bigger, consuming you, and finally it is everything. You feel pain as well as an unspeakable pleasure as the pressure builds and builds, and then...

You scream out exploding the pressure out, and it sends a signal to your husband. He pumps you harder and deeper, faster and faster. At the last moment he wraps his arms round your waist, lifts you off the ground, and grips you tight and still against him. A moment, and you feel the trickle of his cum gushing inside you. You remain motionless with him, your face over the sink, and his body behind you. At this moment, you are one with him. It is the deepest intimacy one human can feel with another. During this moment, the most intense feeling you both have is of serenity, and peace, and being as one. There is no bond more powerful in nature than this.

Sex in marriage is an adhesive. Moments of intense pleasure that have been shared are remembered for years and serve to bond a marriage for life.

Men are hardwired
Men in love want their wives to be satisfied in the bedroom. They will be open to try anything their wives wish them to try if it will make her happy. This desire to please is part of a man's hardwiring. One of the most important hormones dictating a man's behavior is testosterone. It is responsible for both his aggression and his sex drive. Testosterone is also responsible for his protective behavior towards his wife and women in general.

The early history of *Homo Sapiens* had the species living in hunter-gatherer societies. Humans lived as hunter gatherers for hundreds of thousands of years. The civilizations which we live in today are less than 5000 years old. On the timeline of human evolution, civilized society represents mere seconds when compared to the tribal life of our ancient ancestors.

In the tribal communities, men were required to hunt game to bring back to their tribe. They were completely responsible for the subsistence of their communities. As they evolved hunting and killing game, their eyesight improved and they became better hunters.

Males also sought mates and found by sight. There was no real language, and females were selected based usually on nothing more than guttural instinct. Men are visually oriented to this day.

The other behavior that evolved was protective instinct. Males, physically stronger than females, had to fight off both animal and human attackers. This was especially important when their mates were pregnant and when there were children to care for and protect. Finally, and pertinent to this discussion, men are hardwired to please their mates. This is why, when sitting down and discussing sex with your husband, women should try their best not to insult them, or tell them they are inadequate. Being told this sends some men into an unnecessary tailspin of shame and inadequacy.

When wives want to encourage their husbands more in the bedroom and open them up to doing things she wishes to try or has fantasized about, she could engage in "dirty talk." Complementing sexual prowess is always useful. Dirty talk works to convey sexual desire to a husband and open him up to experimentation. Here's a few examples of things a wife can say that really gets men going.

- *I'm gonna come.*
- *Wow, that was the best sex I ever had.*
- *You're so big.*
- *I've never come like that before.*
- *I love how you lick my pussy*
- *You look so sexy wearing that/looking like that.*

They say, "Flattery will get you everywhere," a twist on the popular saying. Flattery is especially potent when it's genuine. A spouse will draw her husband closer to her physically when she lets him know he's doing a good job. It takes little effort but it goes a long way.

CHAPTER 4
Guy Talk

How do you help your wife achieve orgasm? The simple answer is that most women achieve orgasm through clitoral stimulation. Another fact is that some women feel unable to achieve orgasm through sexual intercourse. Less common, some women can achieve orgasm through vaginal stimulation only during coitus.

How can you tell a spouse has had an orgasm? One of the surest ways to know is to ask her. There are subtle physiological changes to her body that will inform you without asking, and they are different in each woman. If you want to understand what happens to a spouse's body, see if you can identify with any of these changes. Note that women usually are not aware of these changes themselves.

1. When you kiss her lips after a very hot and steamy sex session, her lips will be drier than normal.
2. She will have goosebumps on her buttocks or all over her body.
3. Her body temperature cools significantly enough to tell.

Your spouse may exhibit other "tells" than the ones listed. However, to increase the chances she will orgasm, there are many positions that focus on her satisfaction. Three of them are listed here, but more will be discussed later in greater detail.

1. Woman on Top:

In this position, she spreads her legs and straddles her partner's body. His penis penetrates her deeper when she's on top, and she can move up and down it and control the depth of his penetration. When on top, her clitoris rubs against her partner's body. If she can orgasm by both clitoral and vaginal stimulation, this position will give her amazingly intense sensations before and during orgasm.

2. **Doggy Style:** The woman is on all fours and the man stands behind her and penetrates from this position. His penis goes deeper inside her, and if she can orgasm through vaginal stimulation, she stands a great chance of having an explosive orgasm.
3.

3. Modified Missionary: She lies on the bed or a flat surface with her head down. He places her legs over his shoulders and lifts her hips a few inches off the bed. When he penetrates, his penis rubs her internal G spot and produces deep and pleasurable sensations. The most simplistic explanation is that when a woman's vagina becomes engorged with blood, she becomes sexually aroused. The question is, how and when does that happen? More important, how can you bring that about?

One of the interesting things about women (not all, but most), is that they don't actually know what turns them on, until it does. Often, a woman's genital and subjective responses don't agree. There is one obvious tell that men give away when they're sexually aroused: his penis stiffens, engorged with blood. Medicines like Viagra and Cialis work to widen the blood vessels of the male genitals, helping it to erect.

Tests have studied the responses of both men and women to sexual stimuli. Wearing a plethysmograph, in separate studies, men and women were made to watch erotic movies (straight, gay, bisexual, bestiality, etc.) On a superficial level (nonetheless important), the studies show that men respond to visual cues a great deal more than women.

Unfortunately, how women get sexually excited is still a very poorly studied field. One conclusion all researchers come to is that a woman's arousal is more important than her orgasm. Women can be aroused for hours during the day. Signs of female are when blood flows to her genitals, causing her clitoris and vulva to swell. The vagina is now lubricated, and the nipples get hard.

For a woman, sexual arousal can feel like sexual activation or even excitement. Women have a full body experience. It commonly occurs first in the female mind as she has thoughts of sexual desire. From there, is moves to the body. When in a state of sexual arousal women go through several different physiological changes as their mind and body begin to awaken.

Communicate with Her

There is simply no substitute for talking about what each of you like most, and what you don't like, in the bedroom. If you've ever watched pornography, you'd tend to believe a lot of things that really aren't true. For example, some women enjoy cunnilingus, and others feel nothing during oral sex. Some women are self-conscious about you being in between their legs, licking their wet, moist vagina. She doesn't want to spoil the moment, so she won't say anything while she waits patiently until you are done.

Even if you've been married for years, it's a good idea to check in with your wife. Ask her how she feels about oral sex, and many other sexual acts talked about later.

Start out Slowly

While it is not clear *how* a woman gets turned on, we do have a good idea of *what* gets her in the mood.

- Dirty talk
- Your voice speaking softly and deeply in her ear
- Stroking her gently: her arms, thighs, neck
- Kissing her on the lips. There are one **million** nerve endings on the lips
- Your smile
- Touching her knee under the table at a boring event

Note the operative word here is *softly.* Moving too quickly and forgetting about starting her engine first will lead to another night of, predictable, typical and (often boring) sex.

There are things that you do that are not sexual that will stimulate her brain and heat up her body that makes her look at you with sexual desire.

- When you stop wearing dirty jeans and an old shirt and surprise her by dressing up
- Pulling her over to your side of the bed in the morning when you're half awake. The fact that it's a reflex and you're not really awake.
- When you make plans for the both of you, so she doesn't have to think about it.
- When you're watching TV and you pull her legs over your lap.
- When you come up behind her when she's applying makeup or brushing her teeth or something else at the bathroom sink. You wrap your arms around her and kiss her neck.

- You wake up early and make the coffee.
- Any and all displays of affection that are spontaneous and which catch her by surprise.

Fantasy Sex and Real Sex

Having patience, taking your time, engaging in amazing foreplay will lead to a memorable finish. When you watch a typical pornography video, a male porn actor meets a female porn actor.

1. Woman sees man, they may or may not embrace for a few seconds.
2. Woman unzips man's pants/shorts
3. Woman sucks on man's penis for several minutes
4. Man may or may not perform oral sex on woman
5. Woman gets into a sexual position (doggy style, or legs spread apart on the bed)
6. Man prepares to penetrate her
7. They engage in coitus while woman moans and (often) pretends to orgasm.
8. They fornicate in several positions, each of which makes the woman come.
9. Man pulls out penis (or doesn't) and ejaculates somewhere on woman's body.
10. Woman's expression says she just had the best sex ever!

Most, but not all, pornography shows sex without any feeling attached to the act. It is all "fucking and sucking." It's immensely popular because men and women watching porn videos *do* have sexual fantasies as depicted in the video. However, like romance novels and movies, they do not depict the reality of sex.

In our day to day world, we are busy earning a living, working, eating, going to sleep, and then doing the same thing the next day. There is often very little time to get together with your wife to spend time in foreplay. It's important to make time for intimacy, otherwise you are like two ships passing in the night. If you resist taking the time to make physical contact during each day, you being to drift apart and exist in two separate worlds. When you stop communicating with your spouse, she will feel neglected and will withdraw from you.

CHAPTER 5
Finding Time for Sex while Raising Children

Homes with children and pets are always hectic, and the mood is the opposite of romantic. Men often feel neglected, and his wife is constantly attending to the needs of the kids. Finally, the house is quiet, the kids are put to bed and the dog is asleep. Mom and Dad meet in the bedroom and collapse on the bed, exhausted. If sex is attempted, often it's half-hearted at best, giving partners little satisfaction.

This is a situation where the male partner can find ways for him and his wife to make a getaway for a quick tryst. Even when the Mom mildly objects, once you establish a game plan to get together, it will become habitual and your spouse will start to look forward to hot and steamy interludes in the middle of hectic days.

- **Turn a Closet into a Sex Den.** There's nothing like a quickie during a hectic day. Send her a note telling her to meet you in one of the closets in the house. When she meets you there, confused, gift her with her favorite chocolate. She eats for a minute as you work to get her in the mood. She'll appreciate the chocolate and will remember your quick, steamy session together. Especially when you covered her mouth to muffle her ecstatic screams.
- **Schedule time together in advance.** The element of surprise is always a turn on, but sometimes couples need to prepare in advance. Arrange "date nights," hire a babysitter, and spend time together for a few hours. If you have a lover's lane in your town, go and make out in the car. Most cars have room enough for her to mount you after you've pulled down your pants. Within minutes, the windows turn foggy from your hot breath.
- **Close the Door.** One spouse or both have to agree to put their foot down. Draw a bath or take a shower together, agreeing to meet at a specified time. Create a safe space for your children where you can be away for a designated period of time. Restrict young ones to places in the house where they can't get hurt. The darkened bathroom lit only with candles is a wonderful escape, if only for a little while.
- **Talk in Front of the Kids.** Although it's easy to forget that toddlers don't understand what married couples say to each

other, partners should feel free to flirt with each other, kiss each other, and even talk dirty. None of this gets through to toddlers.

- **Shows of Affection in Front of Older Kids.** Partners should show affection towards each other in front of older teenage children. Teens in high school have friends who often come from homes of divorced parents and who are used to seeing their ex-parents fighting and not getting along. These kids belong to a family where the marriage has failed.

Children of married parents who love each other and are in a solid relationship are more   stable because they see the most important adults in their lives getting along. Shows of affection in front of them (even if it embarrasses them), will likely help them establish their own happy and healthy marriage. Children learn most from what they are exposed to in the household.

Part Two - Phenomenal Sex in Marriage
CHAPTER 6
Foreplay

When we think about foreplay, we think of couples touching each
other's bodies, caressing, kissing, oral sex, or anything else that
happens before intercourse. But there is so much more to it than
that. What happens before intercourse is what's remembered most
after you finish. Foreplay can be the hottest part of sex. The old
saying that "the journey is the best part of the trip" is totally
accurate. Foreplay leads to sexual intercourse, and there is
excitement because you both anticipate what's to come. Dopamine is
released in large quantities during foreplay. Intercourse is when the
most powerful orgasms happen, but foreplay makes intercourse
much better.

Foreplay helps couples get closer to each other with displays of
affection, holding hands, kissing and hugging. There are so many
things that can happen during foreplay. Verbal encouragement,
talking, telling each other what you like that the other does to you,
only helps raise the temperature. Sex begins when partners move
from real world concerns to the lovers' realm, when it is agreed upon
in silent understanding that it's time to make love.

The male's penis becomes erect and the woman's vagina lubricates
during foreplay. It is during this time that the entire body becomes
one big erogenous zone. Soft kisses on the neck, cheek, shoulder,
stroking of the inner thighs, touching under the knee, the feet and
head, all respond to touch that moistens the vagina.

Imagine now you are in the living room with your lover, and it's the
evening of a long day, but it's still early. If you enjoy wine, pour a
glass for each of you and turn out some of the lights. If you have
candles, shut off the lights and talk by candlelight. Sit close together
and begin to unwind by talking about the day. You each exchange a
knowing look. Slow down your overactive minds, savor touching, let
it last, and *don't be in a hurry to get to the next step*.

Think to yourselves what you remember most fondly about an earlier sexual experience. Through touching, the zones of sexual stimulation are aroused on partners' bodies. The lips, the most sensitive and most responsive, are the gateway to stimulation other parts of the body. If kissing makes your lips numb, keep it up. Don't rush through it. There's no time limit. The longer time spent kissing, fondling and caressing, the better the sex later will be.

During foreplay, when a woman begins thinking ahead about orgasm, becoming concerned it won't happen, it will make it harder to achieve. Will yourself to accept it and exist only in that precise moment without thinking ahead. Nothing is more liberating that surrendering to the here and now and giving up control.

Your mind is firing with lust and desire, but instead of moving towards intercourse, accept that your desire is rising and feel it become greater and greater. Many women have reported achieving orgasm during foreplay as they allowed their bodies to respond to every stimulus that comes and waiting to feel the next one.

During extended foreplay, a man's penis will begin to throb. The longer time spent pre-coitus, the harder his penis becomes. He may become inpatient to penetrate but it's important not to rush it. The longer he waits to ejaculate, the more intense will his orgasm be.

Taking the time before sexual intercourse is like stepping outside the box. Make yourselves wait and stay in the moment. The feel of your partner's lips takes on a whole new dimension as you slow down and savor newly-discovered softness, moistness, and pressure on your own lips. Experiment with your tongue, explore inside your lover's mouth with it, under the lips, along the teeth, the feel of all parts of the other's tongue. Move your tongue slowly, unlike a propeller. Let the tip of your tongue caress the other's tongues and explore. Before pulling your lips away, gently bite your lover's lip with your teeth, it will drive them wild and make them only want to continue kissing you.

Women: When he moves down to your breasts, softly say, "Slowly. Go slowly." When he does something with his mouth that sends a pleasurable sensation through you, encourage him by letting him know. "Oh yeah, that feels good. Mmmh." Communicating will reinforce his behavior, and he'll know what you like. You should also ask him if he enjoys things that you do.

When giving oral sex to your husband, it may be difficult for him to tell you what he's feeling, so you'll need to ask, "Do you like when I do this?" "How about this?" "Does this feel nice?"

There are some things that you can learn about fellatio on your own. What drives most men crazy has to do with the delaying of orgasm, or extreme teasing. Take his penis in your hand and grip it by the base. Sit between his legs and look up at him. With your tongue, lick below the tip, making your tongue moving in circles as it moves towards the frenulum under the tip.

There are more nerve endings near the tip and under the foreskin below the tip than anywhere else on the penis. It is not necessary to suck it hard like a vacuum cleaner in order to stimulate this area. In fact, a gentle touch with either the fingers or mouth simulates the nerve endings and makes the penis throb.

Men: The two most important words for you to remember are, *be gentle.* It's interesting to note that even though a woman is in the mood, she still needs encouragement and for you to gently stimulate her. There are ways to touch a woman, and there are ways you never should.

In general, women will follow a man's lead in foreplay and if he uses a gentle touch, will likely follow your lead. There are two ways a man enters into sexual foreplay, actively or passively. If a man just goes through the motions, a kiss here, a touch there, as if you're looking at a new car in the dealership, kicking the tires and running your hands along the lines, your partner may respond the way the car you're eyeing does, with absolutely no response.

It's important to keep in mind that the dynamic in "make up sex" is different than when you want to set the scene for sex, or you see she is interested. Even though you are both in the mood, that doesn't mean you should just dive right in. Start by stimulating her erogenous zones, both the common, well-known parts of her body as well as the less commonly touched areas that will add a much-desired spark to your foreplay.

Here is an imaginary scenario told from the point of view of a female in foreplay with her partner.

I love my man. As the years have passed, my love for him has only grown deeper. However, sometimes, our sex life has been predictable. Don't get me wrong, I love having sex with him, it's just that it's always the same. We'd kiss, touch each other for a few minutes, and then have intercourse. I love the fact he finds me attractive and wants to with me, I only want something... different. It seems my wish was heard, because last night, something happened. I was out and my guy was on my mind a lot. I thought about him and my thoughts turned to sex. That happens a lot, but I know that our sex clocks are not always the same.

I got home about a half hour after him and saw him in the living room looking at the TV. I walked up and bent over and kissed him hello and noted he had just come out of the shower and smelled really good.

I walked to the kitchen, the smell of food from the stove. I lifted the covers and looked at the steamed vegetables and the chicken in teriyaki sauce. It looked wonderful and my stomach growled, and I was amazed he had cooked, something he doesn't normally do.

I went over and thanked him, and this time when we kissed, his lips lingered a little on mine and it made them tingle. I was getting worked up already. He got up off the chair and took my coat off for me and told me he'd serve the dinner. Serve dinner? The surprises just kept on coming!

I went and took a quick shower, dried off in front of the mirror. I saw my naked body and craved his touch. I decided to be patient but already felt something in the air, and that alone made me happy – and horny.

I put on a comfortable little outfit that I knew he liked, and decided not to wear a bra or panties, and watch to see if he noticed. I went out to the dining room, and saw the food in dishes on the table, and a bottle of red wine. The only light came from the track lighting on the ceiling which made the room feel smaller and cozier.

We had a wonderful dinner and even though the meal was light, I felt full, but not bloated and sleepy. I wondered if he had planned that... We walked into the living room and talked on the sofa, and now I noticed his eyes straying down to my breasts, and how he watched when I crossed my legs, revealing more of them to him.

This night, he was running the show, and I loved it. We talked about that weekend we spent in the secluded cabin in the mountains, a weekend alone together. It was one of the most romantic times we ever had together, unaware of the cold outside, the warmth of being inside, his arms around me, kissing and touching, and how many times we did it, over and over. Time had stood still, it was only him and me, hour after amazing hour.

The memory of that weekend turned my focus right on him. I moved closer and we kissed, and I felt that electric tingling in my lips again. We kissed for a long time, and I was transported back to the cabin. He kissed my neck and moved up and gently bit my earlobe, sending a surge of pleasure down to my breasts. He moved my head and then kissed the back of my neck, while his fingers tenderly ran through my scalp. I began to forget where we were, all that mattered was how wonderful his gentle kisses were.

We looked at each other, lips close, and embraced again, with even more passion, and his hands brushed against my nipples from the outside of my blouse. They hardened in less than a second, and I sat there as he raised my blouse and cupped my breasts him his hand, hit teeth biting my nipples.

My body began to move and I pulled back and took off my blouse. I was ready, but he wasn't, still cupping and squeezing my breasts, and biting my nipples. I was growing impatient but waited, and realized the more I waited, the more I wanted him inside me. I waited because it was clear he was in control, and that's how he wanted it. I loved it!

He pulled down my little shorts over my feet and now I was naked. Slowly he moved me down onto the couch on my back, and I watched him take off his shirt. My hand reached out to his penis as he undressed, and I felt how hard he was, sending a rush of warmth through my body.

We had both lost weight and got fit, so I admired his naked, sexy body, and I could see him admiring mine. He bent down above me and kissed me below my navel, his mouth moving down. I spread my legs apart, and I was already pretty wet, because of how he had kissed my body. He moved his hands under and squeezed my buttocks before his tongue and mouth touched me. "I love you," he said in the sweetest voice, and that was all I needed to take me over to the other side.

What a crazy, intense night of passion we had, unlike anything we had done together since we got married! My prayer as answered. His gentle touch, his lips on my neck, the way he bit my nipples, how he squeezed my butt cheeks so firmly, his gentle bite on my earlobe, changed our sex life for the better. I don't complain about sex being routine anymore. There's nothing to complain about!

There's a saying that a woman is like a car. It is true only in the sense that she will respond if touched in certain ways. But a car is a machine, and it doesn't have an inner essence, and it doesn't respond like a woman does. A car is a machine, but a woman is a living, feeling creature.

There are so many wonderful sensations couples can have in sexual play, and foreplay is the best way to get there. Think of it as the key that unlocks a door. On the other side are hundreds of different sexual enticements that couples can choose and try together.

By taking the time to explore your partner's body, learning what she likes you to do and what isn't as good for her, you become a sexual expert, and because of the time you've spent finding out what she loves most will increase her interest, and yours as well. Showing her your gentle and patient attention will make her try new things out to please and satisfy you as well.

Kissing: If there is one place where we should take our time when making love, it is kissing. Our lips have over 8,000 nerve receptors and is one of the most sensitive parts of the body. Kisses should always take a long, long time. When kisses are soft and made with feeling, no one wants stop. Nothing else matters when in the middle of a passionate embrace. Everything stops and all that matters are the erotic sensations that arise from mouth on mouth stimulation

Kisses should never be rushed. Feel your partner's lips, their softness and their moistness, explore inside her mouth. Run your tongue along her upper and lower teeth, underneath her lips between teeth and lips. Go along the gums. Gently bite them to end the first kiss and before starting the next. The better you are at kissing, the better lover you will be. It all starts there.

A kiss can make a woman fall in love. Authors throughout history have written of the almost mythical power of a kiss. Kisses should not always be tame. Once in a while, make it more passionate. Unleash your own fiery passion, and she will most likely respond: Push your lover against the wall, raise up her arms and hold them over her head. Press your lips into hers and kiss her like you mean it. Put your fingers in her mouth for her to suck, then take them out and plant a passionate kiss on her lips.

When a woman is comfortable with a partner, she loves to be excited when you touch her body. As a refresher, here are first some of the most well-known areas on a woman's body that gives her pleasant sensations and, in the right environment, brings on her sexual arousal:

> **The nape of the neck**. This area, on the back of her neck, underneath her hair, is sensitive and responds to your soft, dry kiss. By the way, when kissing anywhere on your partner's body, they should be more dry than wet. Wet lips act like a barrier between the feel of your lips and her body, decreasing the pleasure of the touch.
>
> **Lips**. The lips are one of the most sensitive areas on both male and female bodies. There are over 8,000 nerve receptors on our lips. Any foreplay starting with slow passionate kisses will always lead to much, much more.
>
> **Nipples**: Women have different ways they like their nipples touched, but almost unanimously, women love the feeling of hands, fingers or lips being in contact with their nipples.
>
> **Buttocks**: During the day, whenever you walk past your spouse, a gentle smack on her butt is very reassuring, and a sign of affection. Some couples even enjoy making intimate contact in public. If you are in a busy department store and need to separate, a kiss and a gentle touch of her butt signifies your affection for her. Regardless of the crowd around her, you send a message that she is always the focus of your attention, even when you're apart. Most women's rears can withstand a good smack, so go ahead and do it, to let her know you want her.

Inner thighs. During foreplay or perhaps early in the morning when you wake up together in bed, gentle stroking of the inside of her this communicates the message that you desire her. This area of your partner's body is near her genitals, and gentle stroking communicates a powerful message that you want her.

Clitoris. Located above the vagina and at a distance of several centimeters, most women can achieve orgasm almost exclusively from clitoral stimulation. Certain sexual positions stimulate the clitoris during penetrative sex, and these and others will be discussed later.

Aside from these well-known areas of the female body that arouse sexual interest, there are other parts of her body that men are encouraged to try, and may be surprised at the positive response they get.

Armpits. Under the arms the skin is extremely sensitive, and for some, a potent zone of   sexual arousal. Try lightly going up and down on the outside of the armpit before venturing in with your fingers in a circular motion. If you perform this   with your fingers correctly, you won't be told you're tickling her. Using your mouth and lips (not the tongue) is even more stimulating.

Lower stomach. The area below the navel and above the clitoris are extremely sensitive.   Try gently brushing it with you lips before moving further down for oral   sex.

There are many more areas not listen here for you to discover that aren't listed here. Sex with a spouse should be labeled as *making love,* not *having sex.* Marriage vows, depending upon religious denomination or even in the absence of religion, include the words "to have and to hold," "to comfort one another", or "develop physical powers," and so on. Marriage is an agreement to engage in sexual intercourse to please one another, besides its procreative function.

In marriage, sex acts to bind two people closer together, and it will always do so when a husband treats his wife as a lover as well as a partner. Sex together involves penetrative sex, but the road to coitus should be as erotic and stimulating as the act itself.

CHAPTER SEVEN
Let's Talk About Dirty Talk

I was home that afternoon. I had piled up a ton of personal days and my boss insisted I use them. "Use 'em or lose' em," he growled and walked away. So I sat in the living room with the TV on, watching it now and then while I sat with a book in my hand.

I started thinking about my man, how much we've gone through together the last 10 years, how great he was providing for us both, making sure I was always happy and comfortable. I wondered how he was feeling, he had complained of a pain in his shoulder this morning. I don't normally call to bother him, but I felt a pang inside me, and my thoughts drifted right to him.

All of a sudden, I felt horny. It came over me like a wave of desire, and it was a big wave too. I wanted to at least hear his voice. To be honest, I wanted to flirt with my man, maybe even drop a few hints and see where it would go. I looked at the clock, and saw it was his lunchtime. I don't know how he'd take it, he's an open minded guy. But who knows?

All I know is that I wanted him, I wanted to feel his weight pressed down on my body, his lips pressing hard into mine as I feel his passion building and building and...Mmm, yes. These thoughts invaded my mind and made me a little restless. How good it felt when we got together, our naked bodies touching, his kisses hot and wet, all his pent up desire coming out.

It turned me on the way he looked at me sometimes. He thinks he hides it from me, but I always can tell when he's looking at me that way, with his big brown green eyes. Like a lion stalking his prey. I get all worked up when I see the animal in him come alive when he watches me.

I couldn't wait any longer. I picked up the phone and dialed. I wanted him to draw his attention to me and away from his work for a few minutes. I showered early and walked around only in a loose button shirt and panties. My fingers reached down between my legs as I rang his office number.

"Humbert and Mumbert, good afternoon" the receptionist said cheerfully.

"Oh hi. I'd like extension 69 please," I said.

"One moment please." The phone rang as I waited, hoping he would pick up.

"This is Joseph Smith." His voice, professional in its tone, made me think for a moment that I had the wrong extension.

"Joe? Hi," I said softly.

"Hi Anne, how's it going? Enjoying your day off?"

"Yeah, I guess. How is your shoulder?"

"Still hurts a little. A good shoulder massage should help it relax." He dropped a hint for me to do it. "I'll be your masseur tonight, darling. I'll rub you where it hurts. Would you like that?"

There was silence for a moment. I waited.

"Yeah, that would be nice"

"Of course, darling. Anything you want."

Another silent pause and I hoped he was starting to get the picture. My voice was soft, and my mind was racing with sexual thoughts. I wanted him to have the same thoughts.

"Know what I'm thinking about?"

Pretending he didn't know, he said, "No. Tell me." I was grabbing his attention.

"I'd love to feel your body near me, right now."

"You would?"

"Yeah. I was thinking about you sucking on my nipples while I stroked you"

A dead silence. He was getting into listening mode. I waited.

"Tell me more," he said.

"Mmm, honey, I'd love to make your whole face wet with my juices." I was turned on so much now, I just wanted to turn the heat up.

"Really," he said, matter of factly. His voice was arousing me, so I began to stroke my clit.

"Joe, you know what?"

"What?"

"You make me so horny sometimes, I can't stand it." My fantasy was him leaving work early and coming home for an afternoon of hot, steamy sex.

"Is that right?" he asked, his voice softening and becoming deeper. My stroking got faster, making waves of pleasure shoot through my body.

"Know what I'm doing right now, Joe?"

"No. What?" But I knew he knew.

"I'm touching myself... (heavy breathing)... and I'm thinking about how nice it would be... (heavy breathing)... if I could feel your cock inside me right now."

Again there was a long silence, almost too long. I didn't even know if he was still there. His office is always busy, and I thought maybe he hung up to talk to someone there. But I was wrong. He had been listening the whole time.

"I'll be home in fifteen minutes. Don't move. Bye."

Suggestive talking, also known as "dirty talk" is a wonderful way of communicating your desires. It seems difficult at first, sharing your erotic thoughts with your partner. But it's worth it for married partners to feel comfortable doing it. Talking dirty helps cut through the red tape and to get right to the point about your feelings.

Let us imagine a wife is in front of the bathroom mirror, having just come out of the shower. Here, in this fantasy, he walks up to her from behind and catches her by surprise. She smiles as he wraps his arms around her body and kisses her neck. If the moment is right, he can grind into her so she feels him pushing against her buttocks. Even without making a sexual advance, displaying spontaneous signs of affection are almost as important as having a great sex life. However, in this scenario, he is trying to have a moment of intimacy with his partner, and get her into the mood. Men are usually more reluctant to talk dirty to their wives, and instead use their bodies to communicate the same strong message dirty talk conveys. Here, he grinds into her and bends to kiss her neck. Next, he runs his hands up and down her arms, then moves to fondle her breasts and brush his hands over her nipples.

Dirty talk is usually never offending to a partner, and if it is for some reason, there should be a discussion about it. Couples should try and be comfortable when sexual feelings are expressed in words.

This section addresses women, and the fact that talking dirty establishes her feminine powers. In a long term relationship, women can use these powers for the good of her and her husband. There is nothing more a man likes than to be told how much he satisfies you and how good he is in bed. Dirty talk is a form of flattery, and it shouldn't be spoken only in the bedroom. Sexting him when he is at work or saying suggestive phrases during the day wields a woman's feminine power and creates a sexually tense mood that builds until you come together and it is finally released.

Why Women Should Talk Dirty

Talking dirty is a powerful tool – it can turn routine sex into hot, ecstatic sex merely by the power of suggestion. And it isn't only spoken as a prelude to sex. Dirty talk can turn normal sex into a hot and memorable experience he'll anticipate until the next time you are in bed.

Women hold a very influential position in the household. She is an authority, a guide for her partner. She can take him out of a lethargic, disinterested state by making compliments and using her power of sexual suggestion.

As a woman, you can walk up to your partner, when he is either watching TV, or reading, and whisper a provocative message into his ear. You can turn him from a dull, inert state to a state of high arousal. When you kiss him, drop a few words between lip contacts. Men are visual creatures, so when you drop him a sexual suggestion, he begins to visualize it in his mind.

I can't wait until you're inside me. You partner will create a visual of penetrating you.

Can I touch it?

Just looking at you makes me wet.

I couldn't imagine sharing you with anyone. You're so freakin' hot.

Men will usually respond with their own dirty talk, and the visuals combined with the words you speak builds incredible sexual tension fast.

How to Talk Dirty

When starting out, go slowly. If you haven't used dirty talk before and want to start, you will feel awkward if you start with powerful cues. Your partner may misunderstand if the words don't match your authentic personality. Starting out is a time of testing and experimenting for you. You are going to say some phrases and then check his response. *You look sexy today* is only a short distance from being demure. Complements on his attractiveness is a great start. After sex one night, you should try sending him a text about it the next day. Slowly increase your sexy texts so it flows out slowly form you. After a while your partner will become used to your texts and will most likely miss them if you stopped.

Sexting when you're apart brings anticipation about coming home and seeing you. Gentle kisses on the cheek when you first meet each other after work, will turn into tentative kisses on the lips. When he kisses you, make him hold it a second longer each time. Your message is that you want him, in a very intimate way.

Get to know what turns him on and tailor your dirty talk to what he likes. Be aware of what parts of your body he was most attracted to when you met. If he likes your buttocks, wearing tight shorts that advertise your sexy ass, combined with dirty phrases, will be very effective.

Let us imagine your husband is turned on by women who talk dirty but convey a sweet innocence. You could say something like, *I was dreaming about your sexy body and your… well you know, but I was afraid to tell you.* His response will be fast and certain, and he will reply that it's okay and was glad you told him.

Presenting yourself as demure and reserved but in secret you are a wild sexual animal in the bedroom, is very sexy to a lot of men. In fact, most men are not attracted to a woman who is uninhibited to such an extreme that she talks openly about sex and uses dirty words in a boisterous manner. *I bet you have a great dick. You like to f**k?* Woman who come on too strong are a turnoff in general, although there are exceptions.

You can approach your husband and speak shyly to him, as if you're afraid to speak about your hot sexual desires. He responds to your shy disposition, encouraging you to speak. Remaining modest and unassuming, you could whisper in his ear what you want. *Can I touch it?* A phrase like this or *I think you're the sexiest man I've ever met,* can turn a gentle conversation into a hardcore sexual experience in a matter of seconds

It's important to be yourself, more than anything else. Saying phrases that are over the top when you personally are a reserved and quiet woman will make both of you uncomfortable. When you're being yourself and having fun, it comes out as authentic and he will respond positively.

Dirty talk is like "hitting on" your partner, something many women feel uncomfortable doing with a man. Doing it right masks the fact that you're coming on to him. Starting off timidly, then slowly becoming more graphic in your texts and words will go unnoticed, which is exactly what you want.

Dirty Talk Before and During Sex

There are dirty talk phrases you say to build sexual tension and then there are things you say during the act of sexual intercourse, or during foreplay. Talking dirty and suggestively, when you feel comfortable and are enjoying yourself a lot, is extremely stimulating and makes your sexual experience memorable. After a night of hot, passionate sex with your lover, filled with your dirty and suggestive compliments, will be remembered and you can talk about it the next day with him when you're sexting.

To get him in the mood, after you've become comfortable with talking suggestively, start with sexting. When he comes home, he will be thinking of your texts and how they made him fantasize about you. Get together with him on the sofa, or at the kitchen table, or wherever you can be close and comfortable.

I can only think of you naked in bed right now.

You embrace, and the compliment you just gave him supercharges your foreplay. You can continue building the sexual tension.

I want to see your cock.

He imagines he is at home with the sultriest and most desirable lover he's ever met, enjoying you more and more. Keep building up the tension. The slower you advance to real sex in your bedroom, the hotter it will be. Teasing is powerful.

Ooooh, baby. You make me so horny. Mmmmhh.

Now, he starts running his hands all over your body, as you stroke his hardened shaft. Tension is building up, he wants to carry you into the bedroom and throw you down on the bed and have his way with you.

Mmmh, you feel so good. I can't wait to feel you inside me.

The time has come. The two of you go into the bedroom. You're moving from foreplay to intercourse and both of you are thrilled and excited. The dirty talk continues as you embrace and start exploring each other's bodies.

Mmm, your cock is delicious. I could get addicted to sucking it.

Now you're in the heat of intercourse, your bodies moving against each other, he is stiff as cement and you are wet and getting even wetter with each passing second. Now it's time to turn the dirty talk on, full steam ahead.

Your dick is so thick and full. It feels amazing inside me.
I love it when you're hard.
Ohh, baby, harder, deeper!

Ohh, when you pull my hair it makes me want to come.
Harder. I want to feel you deep inside of me.
I'm gonna come!
He penetrates deeper and your bodies move against each other, faster and faster, until finally, you release a deep and powerful orgasm. He comes and comes inside you, or on you. When we're in the moment of hot sex, we often try new things. He may want to spray on your breasts, or pull out of you, and have you suck him to orgasm. There is great acceptance when the sex is hotter than expected.

Afterwards you can continue to compliment his sexual prowess.
My God, honey, you were incredible.
That was so good.
You're such a stud.
Dirty talk spoken after the act is over will be the most remembered. Your partner will have greater confidence the next day, carrying with him the belief that he has satisfied you. You will become an object of his desire. It's important to think back to the words you spoke and which of them resulted in the most acutely intense reaction from him.

CHAPTER EIGHT
Sexual Positions – A Guide for Couples

It is said that variety is the spice of life, and the axiom is never truer than in the marriage bedroom. One of the beautiful aspects of years of marriage is that couples face challenges together, conquer them until the next challenge comes along. Romance novels end when couples live happily ever after in a romantic bliss where they spend day after they enraptured in sexual pleasure, all their desires satisfied. Life is one day after another of hot, steamy, transformative sex. There are no worries about paying bills, nor is there anything else but the bliss of being wrapped in each other's arms all day and night.

Although movies and books about romance paint an idealized picture of marriage that is mostly unattainable (because it's not real), it is quite possible to achieve a state of sexual perfection that's even better. What an intimate couple shares, the intimate details, the silent "knowing" of one another, is rarely captured on screen or in the lines in a romance novel. Long term partners share a deep intimacy, a knowing of each other mentally, spiritually and physically, that no one else can understand. Friends and relatives only have a superficial understanding of the dynamics of your relationship, and in the end, that is for the best.

Couples who love each other have the power of two instead of one. Their deep knowledge of each other acts like a shield. It is a formidable force, a defense against the world. They have what others desire most in love: think of a couple as the most powerful antivirus program made, able to withstand any attacks from the outside that try to corrupt the system, remaining whole despite constant attempts to be hacked.

Many married couples start out with limited resources, live in small apartments and in cities or states that they wish they could move away from. Saving up and moving to the next level, of living in a home with a little land to raise children and have space takes hard work, and the work is accomplished as a team. There are fights but the fighting ends because the bond is strong, and each partner is working towards a common goal.

Maybe a husband works for a time in manual labor, or the wife works in an entry level position while spending time improving her education in her spare time. There are hundreds of scenarios, but they all have in struggle that's accompanied by great stress that threatens the relationship from time to time. Couples know about the threats and will either give into them, or they will fight back as a team. There is no better way to resist than binding closer together through intimacy, and by making time to be together as much as possible, problems that seemed insurmountable are overcome with ease. The most powerful tool a couple has to ease each other's stress is sexual intimacy.

At its most basic, sexual intercourse occurs when the male penetrates the female, and one or both partners achieves orgasm. One of the most popular positions is missionary, the male on top of the female, penetrating her as his body makes contact and rubs against her clitoris. Missionary is a good position, but when other sexual positions are added to your lovemaking, both partners find other ways to excite and pleasure each other, many of them much more satisfying than performing missionary by itself.

Earlier we spoke about the erogenous zones on each partner's body. But these areas are on the outside of the body and are excited prior to intercourse, in preparation for stimulation of the *interior* erogenous zones.

The most important erogenous zone that has not been mentioned, is the one from which all the others come. It is the brain, and when it is properly stimulated, the body becomes one complete zone of sexual arousal for each partner. Different sexual positions stimulate the brain which then brings alive nerve receptors in areas on, and in the body that were not awoken until then.

Many couples are familiar with positions like missionary, 69, girl on top (cowgirl), doggystyle and spooning. Here is a basic description of some of the more popular positions.

69. This sexual position is performed before intercourse. It's a wonderfully stimulating way to prepare for coitus because if helps prepare the genitals and increase physical sensations prior to sex. In this position, each partner forms what can be visually seen as the number "69" when the mouths of each partner comes into contact with the other's. There are several angles in which to perform position 69.

In one, the man lies on his back on the bed, and his partner is on top of him. In this way, she has full access to his penis. She can take it into her mouth and withdraw it as she wishes. She has the freedom of movement to use her tongue to lick him under the tip (frenulum), and to stroke it with her hands and fingers.

The man underneath has her vagina and clitoris in close proximity to his mouth, but with less space. He can take hold of her buttocks, grab her thighs while stimulating her with his mouth and tongue.

Another way to perform 69 is side by side, which allows almost the same amount of free movement for her but also allows much more for him. This is an intimate way of performing the position, because aside from being very comfortable for both partners, there is more space to touch each other's bodies and genitals. Soon after starting, things heat up as her hips and his begin moving back and forth, and in the process, her genitals become moist and ready and more blood flows to is penis, making him even harder.

Another variation that's less common but more satisfying for him is when he is on top. Not only does it allow for the most available space for his mouth contact with her genitals, the angle of insertion stimulates the sensitive part of his penis differently, increasing the pleasurable sensations he receives, due to the angle of placement of his penis inside her mouth.

Spooning. This is a position couples do during intercourse. Like the 69 position, it can be performed at several different angles, and each angle stimulates one partner differently than the other. What's nice about spooning is that it allows for full body contact. The feet, buttocks and legs, and his stomach contacting her back, make this one of the more intimate sexual positions.

In one spooning position, he can lie behind his partner and penetrate her with harder thrusts. Wrapping his arm around her, or holding the side of her hip, he thrusts freely until he ejaculates.

A different way to spoon is doggystyle. This position provides more intense stimulation to her. To do this, she curls her body and slides her feet back, while he holds her hips. He is behind her, and the penetration is deeper and greatly satisfying to both partners.

Lastly, she can lie on her back atop him completely supine, as he penetrates her from below. During penetration he comes into contact with a higher place inside her, near the G spot. She can press her legs together firmly for a tighter feel.

Doggystyle

The woman is on all fours and the men is behind her. He can hold onto her hips as he moves in and out of her. Most women enjoy this male-dominant position; his penetration is deep, more depth than most other conventional positions. The angle at which he moves inside her is ideal for making contact with her G-spot.

With some practice, especially trying different angels of penetration, doggystyle can almost always stimulate her G-spot. An interesting variation of doggystyle is trying the missionary position, but in reverse. Doing this makes penetration feel even deeper, giving an even better chance of coming into contact with her sexually responsive internal area.

Here, she lies down on the bed face down, and raises up her hips slightly. He then inserts into her from above, usually by kneeling (both partners are on the bed). With practice, he will be able to move his body down to lie on top of her back during intercourse.

In this position, however, it is up to the woman to make sure his penis hits all the right spots. She is not completely supine on the bed; her hips are raised a bit off the mattress. She moves her hips back and forth, towards him then away, closer to the bed. She should also try moving to the left and right. With a little practice, moving her hips and keeping in rhythm with his penetration, he will make contact with her G-spot.

From this vantage point, the couple can make it more intimate. She can move down and become completely supine and face down, while her partner straddles her buttocks with his thighs. He spreads her lower butt apart and penetrates. Here she only needs to move her hips if she wishes to, but as he penetrates her and squeeze her buttocks, he will bend over forward, reach underneath and squeeze her breasts, and with practice, he can reach down and kiss her without interrupting coitus.

One night, try performing doggystyle and its two alternatives in tandem. Start with her on all fours and him behind. Then she moves down with her hips still raised a little, moving back and forth. Last, she lies down in a supine face down position while he squats on her from above. Both should achieve orgasm as they "play" through these steps.

A Variation of the Missionary Position

The missionary position is one of the intimate ways to make love. Partners can look at each other during coitus, can kiss and touch each other's bodies the whole time they are "conjoined." Men can usually achieve orgasm in a missionary position.

An alternative way to perform this position is to begin as you and your lover normally do. As you continue, the male can move up, his head and shoulders going over his wife's, his whole body moved forward about six inches. His body now can rest on his partner's upper chest instead of her abdomen. It should be noted here that extra husky men should take care in pressing their weight on their partners, checking with her when trying it out.

His penetration will not be as deep. However, the angle of his penetration has changed, and now the root (base) of his penis makes more direct contact with her clitoris. She can feel the change within seconds, as the rubbing of his stem against her clitoris starts sending waves of pleasure through her body. If he can maintain this position and keep up his thrusting, it is likely she will have a powerful orgasm.

During sex, men should keep their ears open and be good listeners. He should be able to tell when his lover is close to an orgasm and keep up with her progress in getting there by listening. After a point where he believes she has come, he can then move back down to his original missionary position and continue thrusting until he ejaculates.

Your positions begin with missionary > adjusted missionary (female orgasm occurs) > missionary (male orgasm occurs).

Woman on Top (Cowgirl and Reverse Cowgirl)

This position yields the most satisfaction for her. During penetration, he goes deeply inside her. Cowgirl and revere cowgirl can be performed in many different ways. Couples can do it in bed. He is stretched across the bed lying down. She straddles him, her thighs spread over his legs. From this position, she usually assists him in finding her entrance.

She experiences sensual and erotic pleasure through her body by the action of her hips which gyrate up and down along his shaft. She can move her body forward, and the sensation inside of her changes as she leans back further, or moving to the sides of him. Achieving an orgasm for the female is very easy in this position.

Reverse cowgirl offers different internal sensations for her. The angle of his member has changed and as he thrusts, the tip pushes toward the front of her body. This can produce sensational orgasms for her as the tip of his penis rubs against her G-spot. She can also rub her clit while he thrusts into her from behind, her back to him.

Seated Cowgirl

For a more intimate experience, couples can sit up at the end of the bed. He enters her and as he thrusts he touches her body. He wraps his arms around her and holds her close. He thrusts and she gyrates on top of him. Couples are face to face and can embrace and fondle each other. This is one of the most intimate sexual positions, allowing couples to gaze at each other during intercourse. Their bodies are close, the weight of her pressed onto him, thighs touching. Couples can touch each other, the woman, hands free and sitting on top of her partner can fondle her own breasts, or he can bend his body forward and suck on her nipples and squeeze her breasts.

The male's penis penetrates deeper in this position. Because of the comfort offered in this position, couples can stay at this for a long time. He can lift up her buttocks if he wishes, squeeze them and playfully smack them.

The fondling and touching, kissing, squeezing and biting that is possible in the seated cowgirl position helps to bring on hard, intense orgasms for both partners. Experiencing intimate feelings during sex and the likelihood both couples will orgasm, eye contact and touching all over their bodies, makes this a great position to try.

Wheelbarrow Sex Position

The wheelbarrow position requires the woman have the strength necessary to keep her palms down on the bed or floor while the man holds her in midair by her hips. It's a "male dominant' position since he controls the woman's body. It allows him to feel the deepest penetration. The position is like doggystyle.

She situates herself on her hands and feet. He lifts her up by the pelvis. Next, for support, she wraps her legs around his waist and thighs. He holds her and upon insertion is able to go very deep. The man is in control throughout the time spent in the position.

There are hundreds of sexual positon and some extremely intimate ones in the *Kama Sutra,* an ancient Hindu text which lists hundreds of positions and their function. One of the most interesting found in the book is the **Lotus Position.**

Performing this position has him sitting cross-legged, and she sits on top of him. Partners are face to face. He thrusts slowly into her. A slow, constant rhythm is established. This position isn't intended for fast thrusting, but rather a slow building of sensation which progresses to an intense level of physical arousal, ending with deep, satisfying orgasms.

Slow movement is what she responds to, as the gradual rocking and grinding of the bodies stimulates the clitoris. It is fascinating and highly suggested for couples to try together because it is both intimate and immensely satisfying.

There is nothing better than trying out new ways to relate to each other on a deep, erotic level. The expression of raw carnality is best between two people who know each other well, their personalities and their bodies. Over time, experimentation yields knowledge for each partner about the other. Knowing what satisfies your life partner means that as the years pass and aging sets in, sex doesn't have to end. It can go on and on.

Most humans can perpetuate their sex drives throughout the course of their lives. Staying healthy and moderately fit, sex can be as satisfying at age 18 as it is for those in their 80s.

CHAPTER NINE

Sex on the Other Side of the Tracks

There are individuals and couples who seek people of like mind to engage in sexual activities that many believe are either perverse or are only performed by sexual deviants. Out in the world are people who have fixations on certain body parts, and achieve sexual release through stimulation from contact with that part. This kind of behavior is difficult to understand for those who do not have these cravings.

Aside from fetishes, there are many people, some of whom may even be your neighbors, who engage in and enjoy some form or other of BDSM. BDSM stands for "Bondage Discipline Sadism and Masochism," and has gained popularity recently through a fictional book and film loosely based on BDSM activity.

Like everything else, there are some types of sexual behavior in BDSM practice that are similar to conventional sex, while other sex acts go to extremes that, like fetishistic behavior, might be hard to understand.

Close to conventional sex is *rough sex,* which is passionate sex taken to an extreme. Partners, especially females, experience a level of pain that does not occur in conventional sex acts. They enjoy it a great deal. During the sex act, women will have their hair pulled hard, their buttocks spanked almost to the point where welts cover the area. They are treated without gentleness. Much of the experience is a mixture of pain and pleasure. Partners who engage in rough sex enjoy the experience, becoming a part of their sexual routine in their marriage. They have intimate, passionate sex on one occasion and rough sex on the next.

BDSM sex often involves bondage, where a male partner binds the female, either with rope or leather cuffs, to a bed, or shackled in uncomfortable body positions for hours, and achieve sexual release upon being freed and engaging in sexual intercourse. The roles can be reversed as well, with the man being bound by the female.

Dominance and submission involves a dominant and a submissive partner, who is under the complete control of the dominant partner and who must do what he or she tells him or her to do. For some, this lifestyle is round the clock and year round. The dominant/submissive relationship may only take place during sex as well. There are also women who choose to be slaves rather than submissive. The are under the complete control of their Master and have no freedom except that which is granted by their Master. Slaves find the complete surrender to a partner comforting and also sexually arousing.

These lifestyles have made some who do not live in it curious as to what it would feel like to lose complete control of your body, and yourself. Some bondage sex positions have been portrayed in films, often in a negative light. But this is not always the case. Classic films such as *Belle de Jour* and *The Night Porter* examine BDSM practices in a mature manner.

Films and popular culture have referenced being tied to a bed, and perhaps blindfolded with a gag placed in the mouth. There is nothing wrong with exploring this as sexual role playing, where the couple can imagine that the tied up person has been kidnapped, and is being "questioned" by her captor. If she responds correctly, she is rewarded, but if she does no tell the truth, she is punished.

This brings up the idea of *role playing* in a relationship. There are many ways to do this, and some of it is truly fun and stimulating. One partner can be a doctor, examine and probing his patient, or one can be bound to a chair and interrogated by their partner. The tied partner may be teased relentlessly by the other, and these can be fun as well as erotically stimulating.

In a marriage, the only boundaries couples have are the ones they set themselves. What happens in the bedroom is only the concern of the married couple, who can be as free with each other to explore and experiment as both decide is acceptable.

CHAPTER TEN

Keeping Sex Hot and Strong in the Bedroom for Decades

Sex in marriage only ends when we choose it to, or when there are debilitating health issues. Even then, there are many ways to be sexually intimate that don't involve intercourse, but even then, coitus can be achieved with drugs and creative thinking.

Couples who have been together for decades have a deeper understanding of each other. They have lived and experienced life together, deep sadness and incredible joy. On another, they have an intimate understanding of each other that younger people cannot possibly understand. Couples celebrating 30, 40 and 50-year anniversaries have what most of us strive for – a life partner with whom to go through life, and share their experiences and their viewpoints, and to always be there for each other.

This deeper level of understand thing they have for each other should easily translates to the bedroom. Sexual relations in older couples, who've learned about each other's bodies, can have even more intimate and satisfying sex than newlyweds.

Over the years, married couples have raised children, watched them go off to live their own lives away. Dedicating decades to their children, the sexual spark they had often fades because there was less and less free time.

One of the ways couples can reignite the spark is to get back in touch with their own sexuality. It is still there, but it is has become dormant from lack of use. Partners should go to places they've never been to before and spend time getting to know each other sexually again. They will be surprised at how easy it is to reestablish erotic romance. After all, it had been practiced for years until the children became their primary focus.

Experimentation

It is not possible to over emphasize the critical importance of trying new things. Even if you have wonderful chemistry together performing the same sexual positions, take the time to try new ways to stimulate and please each other, because the day will come when those familiar positions won't deliver the satisfaction you crave. Push the boundaries of your comfort zones by introducing sex toys into the sexual mix. There are couples' vibrators that please both partners.

Be spontaneous. Plan a surprise for you partner. Leave flowers for her and include a note with them that she is to meet you at an address you leave. The mystery will be intriguing and exciting for her. You decide where the meeting place will be, such as a spa, a 5-star hotel, or the airport, where you'll both go on a trip to another country.

Stay Best Friends

Humans are not capable of telepathy, so communication, talking and finding out what issues are affecting your partner, and how you can help to solve it. Always be there for your partner. He or she should be the primary focus of your life. Rewards come later in life when you've always kept your partner in the forefront of our mind, no matter how many miles are between you.

If you travel on business, make sure to stay in touch and let your partner know you're alright and that you are thinking about them. Send gifts to your loved one from wherever you are or bring home something that will connect your partner to the place you were staying.

No matter how many friends we have in our lives, the truest friend and the best, is our partner. They have had to deal with us on our worst days When other friends may have abandoned you, our partner stuck with you through it all.

If you walk past your wife somewhere in the house, make physical contact of some kind. If she's cooking a meal, go past and pat her buttocks and kiss her cheek. Help out now and then by doing the shopping, and even try doing the laundry from time to time. She may laugh at the difficulty you have folding clothes, but in her heart, her love for you just grew ten times stronger. You showed that you cared about her.

Try going out and doing things together as much as possible Breaking the routine and experiencing new things together binds a marriage.

Have sex even at times you are not in the mood, and your partner is. Endure it for their sake, and they will remember it when it is your turn to have sex with them. They will do it for you because you did it for them.

If retired, partners can spend hours together in an embrace in a swimming pool, hold and touching each other. Although this isn't sexual intercourse, it is highly intimate and can most likely lead to erotic adventure in the bedroom.

Printed in Great Britain
by Amazon